FOR MY MOTHER

For my mother,

with love and gratitude,

From:

Date:

FOR MY MOTHER

✳

A KEEPSAKE *of* THANKS
& MEMORIES *of* GROWING UP

by Jessie Chapman

STEWART, TABORI & CHANG

New York

For my mother,
Margaret McKee Chapman

And my mother's mother,
Jessie Rhedemeyer McKee

❋

Jessie McKee Chapman

Published in 2005 by
Stewart, Tabori & Chang
115 West 18th Street
New York, NY 10011
www.abramsbooks.com

Canadian Distribution:
Canadian Manda Group
One Atlantic Avenue, Suite 105
Toronto, Ontario M6K 3E7
Canada

ISBN: 1-58479-409-7

Designed by Laura Lindgren

The text of this book was composed in Oneleigh, Sackers Gothic Light, and Sackers English Script.

Printed in China
10 9 8 7 6 5 4 3 2 1
First Printing

Stewart, Tabori & Chang is a subsidiary of

LA MARTINIÈRE
GROUPE

INTRODUCTION

I always wished my mother had created a baby book for me. With four children to care for, she abandoned this tradition after child number one. As child number three, I didn't stand a chance given her busy schedule. Nevertheless, I loved hearing my mother tell stories about me when I was growing up—moments I was too young to appreciate or remember. They made me feel wanted and secure.

One day, I was musing on the lack of a baby book again. What if I made a book for my mother that shared memories of my childhood and growing up from my perspective as an adult? In effect, I would create a "baby book in reverse."

So I made her an album—*For My Mother*—for her seventieth birthday. (My two brothers and sister participated too.) It was a big hit. She cried and told all her friends. And I told mine. That's when something very interesting began to happen. Friends started to tell me about *their* mothers and *their* memories of growing up. Almost everyone had a story they wanted to share. We all have mothers. And whether we consider her our best friend or have a relationship that's more formal, we feel connected. The stories may be unique, but the feeling is universal.

As my mother now knows—thanks to her album—one of the lessons I'm most grateful for is her teaching me good manners and explaining that simple gestures like saying "thank you" go a long way. That's what *For My Mother* is all about. This album brings mothers and their children closer. I hope you have a lot of fun sharing memories.

✻

MEMORIES AND REFLECTIONS

These are some of my most enduring memories of growing up. Both large and small, these moments made a big impression on me.

My first memory is . . .

I remember when you taught me how to...

One of our funniest moments together was...

I liked to watch you while you were…

You always impressed me when...

My biggest pet peeve about something you made me do, wouldn't let me do or have was…

One of the "bad" things we had fun doing together was...

Something "bad" I did and never told you about was...

PHOTOGRAPHS

The time I missed you most was...

I thought you were so glamorous when...

i think you are glamorus all the time.

Words and expressions you often used were...

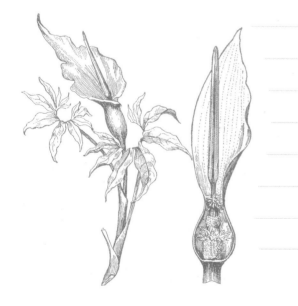

Something you said that really shocked me was...

One of the best and most formative experiences that happened to me was...

My proudest accomplishment was...

Can you name my favorite book, place to play, or gift as a child? You may be surprised! And we'll have fun looking back together.

My favorite family pet was…

well Jake (he has been our only real pet.) He is
energetic, but we love him. Alot of the time
I think that he and his bone stink!

My favorite perfume that you wore was...

*M*y favorite holiday or birthday present was…

*M*y favorite birthday dinner and cake were…

*M*y favorite foods you cooked were…

My favorite photograph of me growing up is...

My favorite family photograph is…

My favorite photograph of you is...

PHOTOGRAPHS

*M*y favorite children's book was...

My favorite places to play were...

My favorite place in our home was...

*M*y favorite grade in school was…

My favorite way to spend time with you alone was...

My favorite family holiday tradition was...

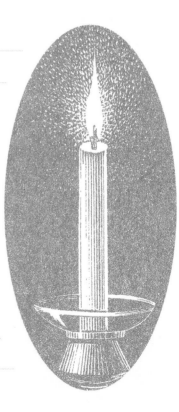

My favorite family vacation was…

$\mathcal{M}$y favorite color was...

GRATITUDE AND
LESSONS LEARNED

We may not have always agreed on things while I was growing up, but I want you to know now how much I appreciate what you've done for me.

I'm glad I listened to you when…

I wish I'd listened to you when…

you told me to transfer to P. C. S.

The time I needed you most and you were there for me was...

_____

_____

_____

_____

_____

_____

_____

_____

The best advice you gave me about friendship was…

You *influenced my personal view of faith by...*

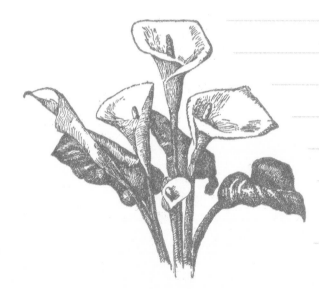

Some things you know how to do well that I wish I had learned are...

PHOTOGRAPHS

Some things I was comfortable telling you but never anyone else are…

Thank you for not getting mad at me when…

_____

_____

_____

_____

_____

_____

_____

_____

The "bad" traits in me you pointed out so I could improve were...

_____

_____

_____

_____

_____

_____

_____

_____

The good traits you saw in me and reinforced were...

The traits I'm most grateful to have inherited from you are...

The most powerful lessons you ever taught me were…

Now that I'm a parent, I finally appreciate that the hardest part of raising children is...

The best advice you gave me about how to be a good mother is...

The nicest thing you did for me when I had children of my own is...

You are a wonderful grandmother because...

ABOUT THE AUTHOR

Jessie Chapman never received a baby book from her mother, so she decided to make a "baby book in reverse" for her mother. She was grateful to discover that others loved the idea too, but they didn't have the time or creative confidence to create their own albums from blank pages. Chapman realized that more people would give and receive personalized keepsake albums if all they had to do was "fill-in-the-blanks." *For My Mother* is Chapman's first book in a series. *For My Friend* will be published next. (She hopes to receive many of them.)

Share stories about creating or receiving this album
at www.formymother.net